Joanie's House Becomes a Home

by **Donna Latham**
illustrated by **Catherine Blake**

PEARSON

Scott
Foresman

Editorial Offices: Glenview, Illinois • Parsippany, New Jersey • New York, New York
Sales Offices: Needham, Massachusetts • Duluth, Georgia • Glenview, Illinois
Coppell, Texas • Ontario, California • Mesa, Arizona

Every effort has been made to secure permission and provide appropriate credit for photographic material. The publisher deeply regrets any omission and pledges to correct errors called to its attention in subsequent editions.

Unless otherwise acknowledged, all photographs are the property of Scott Foresman, a division of Pearson Education.

ISBN: 0-328-13389-2

7 8 9 10 V0G1 14 13 12 11 10 09 08

What is a home? It's more than an apartment or a house. A home includes the special things in it. You might have books, toys, and games in your room. You might have a favorite chair in the kitchen. Those things help you feel good.

Sometimes, people need to move to a new home. Moving can be exciting. But it can make you homesick, too.

Let's meet Joanie Chen. She is eight years old. She is packing. Her family is moving to a new city in two days.

Packing Up

Joanie and her Mom are packing. But Joanie doesn't want to move.

"All my things are here. So are my school and my friends," Joanie says.

"You'll make new friends," Mrs. Chen says. "And you'll like the new school. We are taking *all* your things. That way, you'll feel right at home."

The Chens are saying farewell to their old house in San Francisco, California. They are ready to go. First, they packed all their things into boxes. Now, moving men load the boxes and the furniture into the truck. They empty the entire house.

Sometimes people move very far. The Chens are moving all the way from San Francisco, California, to Boston, Massachusetts. That's a move from one side of the United States to the other!

Moving men will drive the truck from California to Massachusetts, right up to the driveway of the Chen's new home. But the Chens are at the airport. They're taking a plane.

"I can't wait to see our new home!" says Jimmy.

"I can," says Joanie.

"Aren't you curious what your new home will be like?" her Mom asks.

"Will my bed be there?" Joanie asks.

"It's still in the moving truck," Joanie's Mom says. "The movers will take three days to drive it."

Joanie watches raindrops spill down the plane window. She feels sad inside. It started when she was packing. It got stronger at the airport.

She is filled with memories of her San Francisco life. She already misses her school and playing soccer with her friends. She misses the big hills of the city. Most of all, she misses her room, with all her things. She wonders if she'll ever feel at home again.

"This is not a good way to move to a new home," Joanie says to her Mom after some thinking.

"Why?" asks her Mom.

"We don't even have our beds," Joanie says. "What will we sleep on?"

"Don't worry," her Mom says. "We'll pretend we're camping. It'll be fun."

"Right," Joanie says.

First, the Chens packed up their things. Then, moving men packed the boxes and furniture into a truck. The truck is still on the way to Boston. None of the Chen's things will be here for another two days.

"I can't believe this plain empty house is our new home!" says Joanie.

"Don't worry," says Mom. "We will fill it soon enough."

"You bought me a plant!" Joanie says.
It makes her happy to see it.
   "And when all of our things come
we will make this new house into a real
home," Mom says.

Where Does This Go?

Did you ever think about where you live? Each room is used in a different way. Every corner of your home plays a part.

We can use a floor plan to see how the Chen's new house is set up. A floor plan is a map of the house, its rooms, walls, and windows. Why is a floor plan important? So you know where to put everything! Mrs. Chen used a floor plan when she described the new house to Joanie.

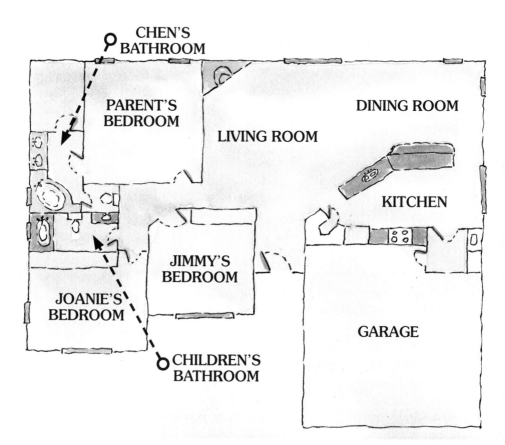

CHEN'S BATHROOM

PARENT'S BEDROOM

LIVING ROOM

DINING ROOM

KITCHEN

JIMMY'S BEDROOM

JOANIE'S BEDROOM

GARAGE

CHILDREN'S BATHROOM

"Hello Mr. Chen," the moving man says. "Where do you want your piano?"

"I didn't know we even had a piano!" says Mr. Chen.

"Bring it in the living room please," says Mrs. Chen. "And thanks!"

What do you think goes in
Mr. and Mrs. Chen's room?

Joanie's bed, clothes, desk,
plant, books, soccer poster,
soccer ball, soccer trophy,
desk, chair, sneaker
collection, and photos go
in Joanie's room.

Jimmy's bed, clothes,
toys, games, books,
dresser, table, chair,
scooter, and helmet
go in Jimmy's room.

The couch, easy chair, piano, bookcase, lamps, and TV go in the living room.

The table, chairs, and ceiling lamp go in the dining room.

The moving men have one day to empty the truck and fill the Chen's whole house. It's a long day!

A New House Becomes a Home

Moving is a big change. You leave your home and you have to start all over again, from scratch. But the moment you bring something of yours into a new place, you're making yourself a home.

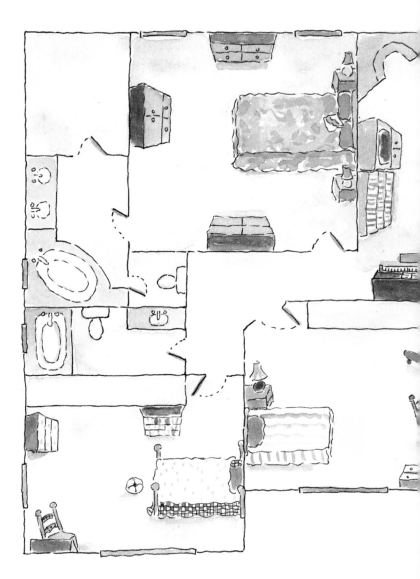

How are the Chens doing? They've filled their home with their things. Do you think Joanie feels better about her new home now?

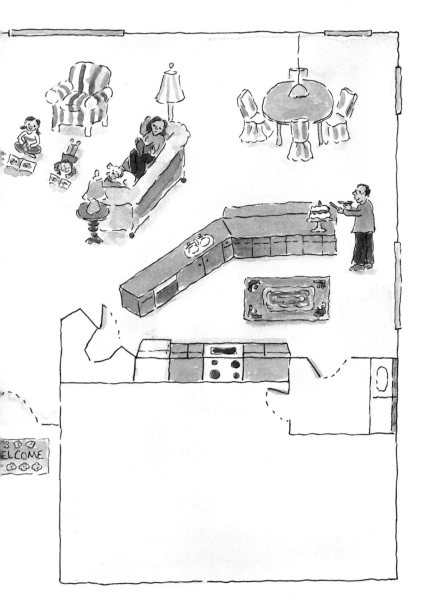

Joanie's New Room

Let's see how Joanie's doing. She finished her room. She and her Dad painted the walls yellow and hung up her soccer poster. Her friends from soccer practice in San Francisco sent her a team picture. They signed their names on it. Joanie and her old friends stay in touch with e-mails. She doesn't feel as far away from them as she thought she would.

What else is different about Joanie's room? She's got a new friend visiting.

"Your room is really comfortable," says Kelly, Joanie's new friend.

"Thanks!" Joanie says. "Now it feels like home. My parents promised we would make this into a real home. But I was too mad about moving to believe them."

"We moved here too—from Texas," Kelly says.

"Don't you get homesick?" asks Joanie.

"Well, it's like what you say. The new house can be homey too. And the ice cream in Boston? Delicious!"

Coast to Coast

The Chens moved from one coast of the United States to another. A coast is a strip of land bordering an ocean. The Pacific Coast, where San Francisco is, runs along the Pacific Ocean. The Atlantic Coast, where Boston is, borders the Atlantic Ocean.

The Chens flew from coast to coast. But what if they had traveled by boat? They would have sailed south along the Pacific Coast to the Panama Canal, in Central America. The canal is about fifty miles long. After sailing through it, they would have continued north along the Atlantic Coast to Boston. How would you rather make the coast-to-coast trip, by plane or by boat?